25
EASY TO GROW
VEGETABLES

in any size plot

25
EASY TO GROW VEGETABLES

in any size plot

•

HENRY CHARLES

LONDON
W. FOULSHAM & CO., LTD.
New York Toronto Cape Town Sydney

W. FOULSHAM & CO., LTD.

Yeovil Road, Slough, Berks., England.

ISBN 0 – 572 – 00913 – 5

Made and Printed in Great Britain by
Bristol Typesetting Co. Ltd., Barton Manor,
St. Philips, Bristol

CONTENTS

Acknowledgement

Cover and Cartoons by Mike Jupp

INTRODUCTION

No matter how small your garden may be it is still worth while to use part of it for growing vegetables. They taste better than the ones bought in the shops, do you more good and save you a lot of money into the bargain. It's surprising how many carrots or cabbages you can grow from just one packet of seed costing a few pence a packet. If you are on a diet, whether for health reasons or just because you want to lose some weight, you will find fresh vegetables and salad foods straight from the garden will make it more enjoyable. With the minimum amount of work it's possible to keep the family in fresh vegetables throughout the year. When there's a bumper crop of any one sort, and it's impossible to eat them all while they are still young and tender, you can store them in the deep freezer to use later on in the year to add variety to your meals.

PLANNING YOUR GARDEN

If it is necesary to divide up your existing garden into kitchen garden and flower beds then use a sunny open position for the vegetables. You can screen it from the flower bed, if you wish, by using interwoven fencing which will also protect the young plants from damage by strong winds.

Set aside one corner of the vegetable patch to use as a seed bed. Seed sown in the spring can later be transplanted to the main garden and early plants can be raised in this part of the garden under cloches or glass and transplanted when they are large enough to do well in the open ground. Growing from seed is much less expensive than buying young plants so if you want to save money then a seed bed is essential.

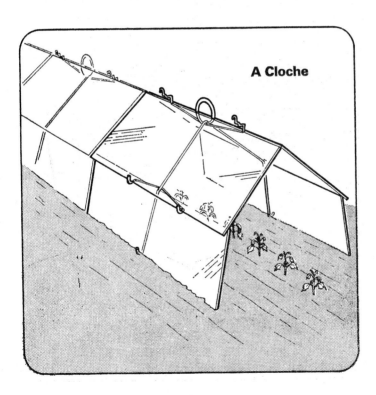

A Cloche

To save having to buy artificial manure make a compost pit. It should be in a sheltered corner and into it should go all your lawn mowings, leaves, decayed vegetable matter and even kitchen waste. It should measure about 4 ft. across with vertical sides and be made in layers of up to 10 inches thick topped with a 2 inch layer of animal manure or a layer of sulphate of ammonia or other nitrogenous fertilizer. Or you can use one of the proprietary chemicals sold for the purpose allowing one handful per square yard.

2" LAYERS OF ANIMAL MANURE OR NITROGENOUS FERTILIZER.

10" LAYERS OF DECAYED VEGETABLE MATTER, KITCHEN WASTE ETC,

4ft. sq.

MAKING A COMPOST HEAP

THE TOOLS YOU WILL NEED

If you are already growing flowers then you probably have most of the tools necessary for growing vegetables. Just check that you have a *Fork* for digging when the ground is very hard, a *Spade* for general digging, a *Dibber* or *Trowel* for planting out seedlings, a *Rake* for levelling off the soil and for covering over newly planted seeds, and a *Hoe* for keeping the weeds down. There are several different *types of hoes*; the *Dutch Hoe*—the push type—is perhaps the most widely used and it's the least back-breaking way I know of dealing with weeds between the rows of plants. There is also the *Mattock Hoe and Fork* which is a double sided tool with a plain blade on one side and a three-pronged fork on the other. Use this for chopping out weeds, earthing up soil around root vegetables or breaking up heavy clods of earth. A *Garden Line* is necessary to keep your vegetables in neat straight rows. You can make one from a length of twine or string and two stout stakes. A *Wheelbarrow* is useful and of course a *Watering can*. I have one with an adjustable spout and a set of different heads so that I don't drown the very small plants when I water them. If you can find room for it on your plot it's a good idea to put an old *galvanized tank* or something similar to collect the rainwater. This is better for the young plants than tap-water, and saves carrying cans of water long distances.

BASIC TOOLS FOR VEGETABLE GARDENING

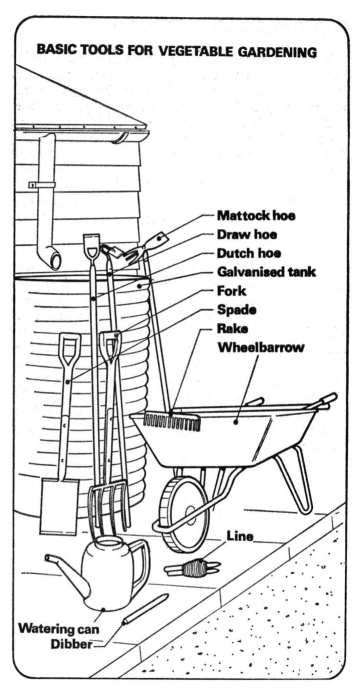

Mattock hoe
Draw hoe
Dutch hoe
Galvanised tank
Fork
Spade
Rake
Wheelbarrow

Line

Watering can
Dibber

METHOD

To keep digging and manuring to an absolute minimum I plan my vegetable garden in four sections. Each year I plant a different type of vegetable in each section so as to make the fullest use of the soil since different vegetables take different things out of it. I find a four-year rotation works the best. I manure it well the first year before planting cabbage and follow this the next year with potatoes and I only have to give it a very light top dressing of manure the following years.

I find that I get the best results by planting root vegetables such as carrots, parsnips or turnips the year after potatoes and follow these with peas and beans in the fourth year.

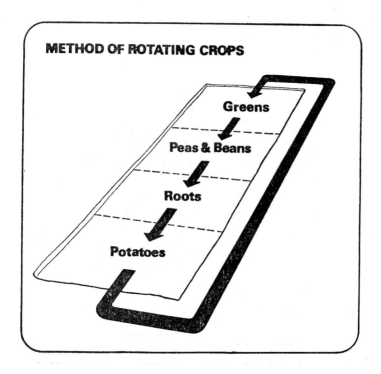

METHOD OF ROTATING CROPS

Greens

Peas & Beans

Roots

Potatoes

Whenever possible I try to stagger the planting of vegetables. For example, I find that if I plant a separate row of lettuce at two-week intervals then I am able to pull fresh lettuce straight from the garden for a lot longer than if I put in three or four rows all at the same time. Peas, beans, radishes, carrots and cabbages can all be planted in succession in the same way. I also plant one crop in between another crop so that while the first one is developing and ripening the other is being picked and cleared out of the ground. It's one way of making greater use of the ground available. In some instances I sow seed in frames, or raise young plants under cloches, and then transplant them when they are big enough to plant out either in beds on their own, or in between other crops that are growing.

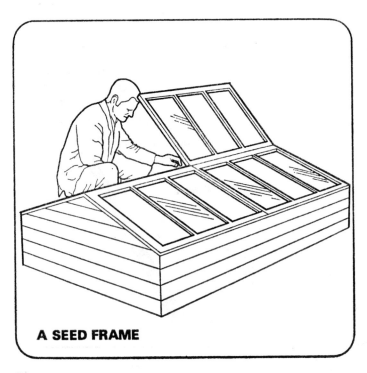

A SEED FRAME

SOIL

Try and find out just what kind of soil you have in your garden since it may be necessary to restore a balance to get the type of soil most suitable for the vegetables you prefer to grow.

SANDY soil is very 'light', open and well drained. It is easy to cultivate, drains readily and its open texture allows roots to penetrate easily. It is very suitable for early crops. To maintain an adequate supply of plant food, however, artificial fertilizers must be applied in small quantities and fairly frequently since they are easily washed out.

CLAY soil is 'heavy' and has virtually the opposite qualities to sandy soil. It is very rich in plant foods and therefore requires only the minimum of artificial fertilizer. It is not suitable for early crops.

CHALK soil is similar to sandy soil in that it is thin and needs a considerable amount of artificial fertilizers. It also dries up very quickly.

PEATY soils are usually very acid and are not suitable for root vegetables. Crops such as lettuce and celery, where quick tender growth is required, produce the best results.
The texture of a soil can be improved by adding soil of the opposite texture, add clay to peaty or sandy soils; peat or sand to a heavy clay soil. Unfortunately, considerable amounts are required to make any real effect so it is only practical in the small garden. It is probably far better to identify the type of soil you have and then plan your crops to suit the soil.

MULCHING is also a valuable method of improving the soil and feeding the plants and also of controlling weeds around growing plants. A good mulch is a mixture of peat, well decayed garden compost, any kind of well rotted natural manure, mushroom compost and even a small amount of sawdust. Clear the ground of weeds before applying the mulch and do not use mulch before mid-April, thus allowing the ground to warm up first, otherwise the plant growth will be slowed up. When it is necessary to water, or to apply liquid fertilizers, allow an additional gallon of water per square yard to wet the mulch.

RECORDS are worth keeping. I find it helps to know how long it takes to grow each different type of plant from the time I sow the seed until it's ready to pick. If you do the same, then you'll find you have all the information to hand when you come to plan out your garden next year.

You will probably find that some varieties do better in your garden than others, depending on the type of soil you have and the position of the garden. The only way to find this out is by trial and error and by keeping a record. Do experiment and plant something new each year, even if it's only a different strain of seed of your favourite vegetable. Don't think that because the gardening books all tell you that you need a particular type of soil to grow a certain crop that it's a waste of time trying it in your garden. I know a chap who grows first class tomatoes in a clay soil with very little attention to them at all and who even manages to get a very good potato crop from his garden even though he doesn't dig it over very thoroughly and doesn't bother to manure it. There's a lot of luck as well as skill to growing vegetables and if you have green fingers you can probably grow anything anywhere. However, since you can only expect to get out of the ground what you put into it there's no harm in clearing the ground after you've finished picking, digging the soil over to allow the air to get into it and freshen it, and then applying slow-acting fertilizer of some kind before planting your next crop. Try to do this in the autumn, then leave the ground fallow and let the frost and snow get at it and they will do most of the work for you.

As well as putting fertilizer on the soil, it is also important to give it a dressing of lime. Each year the soil loses lime steadily and continuously and unless this is replaced the soil becomes acid and sour. The exception is the plot where you plan to grow potatoes next year; this should be well manured but not given any lime.

The most inexpensive method of growing vegetables is from seed. Always buy a good quality brand and follow the instructions given on the packet. Whether you have

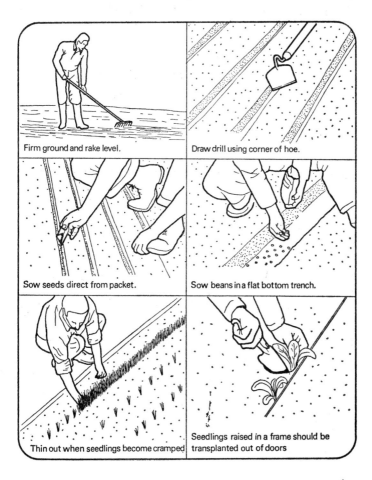

Firm ground and rake level.

Draw drill using corner of hoe.

Sow seeds direct from packet.

Sow beans in a flat bottom trench.

Thin out when seedlings become cramped

Seedlings raised in a frame should be transplanted out of doors sown in the greenhouse, under glass or straight into the open, it is important to thin out the seedlings as soon as they are an inch high and can be handled fairly easily. Unless they are thinned out early their growth will be retarded. Once you have thinned them out water them thoroughly. Keep them well watered if the weather is dry, allowing up to two gallons of water to each square yard. Make sure that seedlings are planted firmly and in the case of peas and beans they should be staked. There are several methods of doing this ranging from the old style of a row of poles running in a straight line, to separate poles at intervals with the plants set around each pole in a circle and trained up strings attached to the pole. Or, you can space poles at six feet intervals with wire mesh fencing between them for the peas and beans to climb.

Vegetables are prone to attacks from certain garden pests and unless these are kept under control an entire crop can

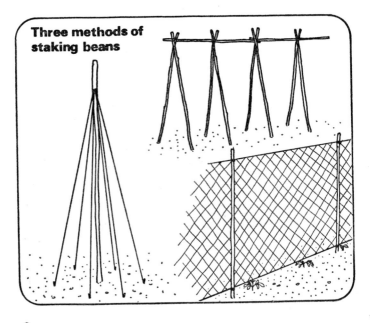

Three methods of staking beans

be ruined. Inspect your vegetable garden once or twice a week from April onwards and treat any affected plants the moment you spot they have been attacked by pests. Spraying is one of the most effective measures and should be carried out immediately and repeated at intervals of about ten days.

PLOT MANAGEMENT AND SEED SOWING

STARTING OFF THE PLOT. Dig a trench out at one end of the plot. Carry the soil to the other end of the plot. It will be needed later on.

SOWING SMALL SEEDS (parsnip, carrot, beetroot, swede, turnip etc.) when fresh manure is not required. Dig back

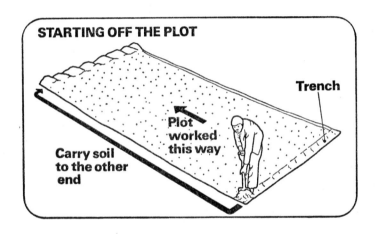

STARTING OFF THE PLOT

Trench

Plot worked this way

Carry soil to the other end

a couple of feet at a time, throwing soil over and forward to leave a level surface. Rake the top soil to a fine tilth. Place the garden-line in place across the plot where the seeds are to be sown. Make a shallow drill with the back of the rake and sow the seeds thinly in the drill. Cover over with fine soil.

SOWING SEEDS OVER A MANURED TRENCH (peas, beans, lettuces, potatoes etc.). Dig back from the previous row to the position of the next row (say 2½ ft.). Place manure or rotted compost in the trench, mark its position and dig back about 18 ins. You are then ready to sow the seeds in the row just prepared.

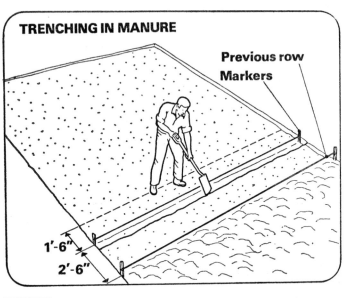

TRENCHING IN MANURE

Previous row
Markers

1'-6"
2'-6"

PESTS AND DISEASES

One of the best ways of controlling pests and diseases is to prevent them getting established in your garden. Keeping the ground clear of weeds and waste, regular digging and hoeing, and adequate fertilizer to ensure good strong plants which can resist attacks, will all help. Crop rotation is also important since if you grow the same crop on the same patch of ground each year this will encourage pests.

The important thing is to inspect your vegetables regularly so that you can deal with any infestation before your entire crop is ruined. Here are the main ones to watch out for:

APHIS. This covers pests known as greenfly, blackfly and

whitefly. Blackfly can be particularly harmful to broad beans and to French beans and runner beans. To keep them under control, dust over with Derris or Malathion.

BIRDS. These can ruin peas and lettuces by pecking out the succulent growing point. Protect them from the birds with black cotton which can be supported on short sticks as soon as the seed has been sown.

BLACK FLY which attacks Broad beans.

Prevent pests and diseases getting established by:- (a) regular digging
(b) using adequate fertilizer
(c) crop rotation
(d) spraying with insecticide & weed killer
(e) burning diseased foliage

CABBAGE APHIS which appear as greyish powder patches.

CABBAGE WHITE BUTTERFLIES. Eggs appear in batches of 20–100 which in a fortnight hatch out into bluish or greenish black caterpillars with yellow markings on back and sides.

FLEA BEETLE which attack Turnip leaves and Cabbages.

LEATHER JACKETS. These are the grubs of the Daddy Long Legs and attack most vegetables.

MILLIPEDE will attack most root crops. Not to be confused with the Centipede which does not harm crops.

PIGEONS. Can be especially troublesome if you grow Red Cabbage but will also attack other green crops in certain areas.

SLUGS which attack lettuces.

SMALL WHITE BUTTERFLY. Lays eggs singly which turn into velvety green caterpillars.

SNAILS which attack lettuces.

WIREWORM which attacks potatoes, tomatoes and carrots. As well as treating with Derris, these pests can also be trapped in an old potato buried underground.

With pests it is usually possible to arrest attack by spraying just as soon as you spot them, but diseases have to be prevented since they cannot be cured. Diseased foliage or

The Woodpigeon

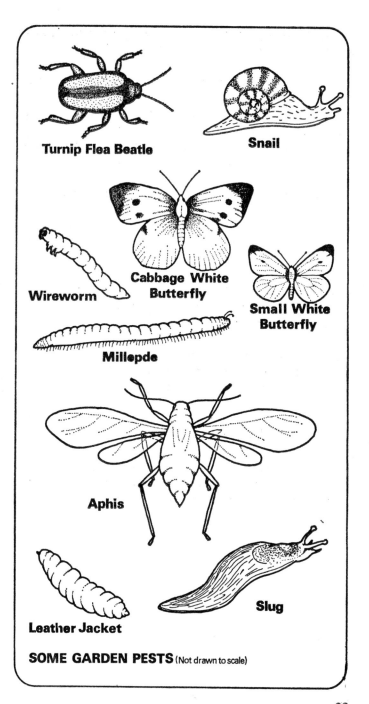

Turnip Flea Beatle

Snail

Cabbage White Butterfly

Wireworm

Small White Butterfly

Millepde

Aphis

Leather Jacket

Slug

SOME GARDEN PESTS (Not drawn to scale)

vegetables should be burned and never left lying around on the ground or even put onto the compost heap.

CHOCOLATE SPOT attacks Broad beans but it is not serious.

CLUB ROOT attacks swedes, turnips, cabbages, Brussels sprouts. The plants wilt and there is usually a large swelling on the roots. To prevent, dip the roots of young plants into a thin paste of calomel dust before planting.

LEAF SPOT attacks celery leaves but it is not serious.

MILDEW shows as a white powder on leaves and stems and can appear on almost any plant. Spray or dust with dinocap.

PARSNIP CANKER usually only attacks Parsnips, the roots rot at the shoulder in winter. By practising strict crop rotation this trouble is usually overcome.

POTATO BLIGHT shows as brown blotches on leaves and stems in June or July but the spores eventually affect the tubers. Spray with maneb or Bordeaux mixture.

TOMATO BLIGHT. This is very similar to Potato blight and should be sprayed in the same way.

WHITE ROT affects members of the onion family. Destroy the plants and next season dust seed drills or planting sites with 4 per cent calomel dust.

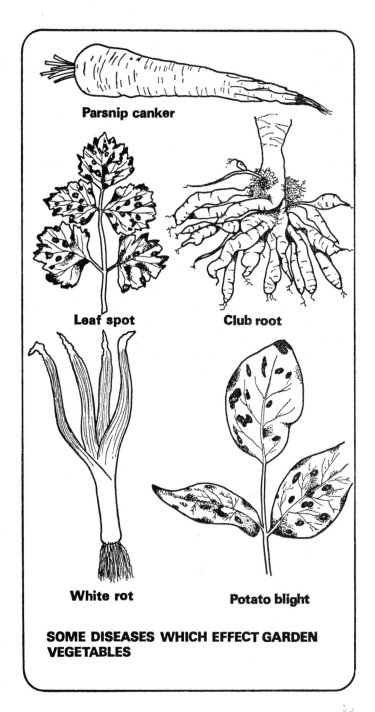

Parsnip canker

Leaf spot

Club root

White rot

Potato blight

SOME DISEASES WHICH EFFECT GARDEN VEGETABLES

FERTILIZERS

As I have already said in an earlier part of this book, you can only expect to get out of your garden what you are prepared to put into it. This means that in order to gather good crops you must be prepared to feed the ground. Your compost heap should provide the bulk of the general fertilizer you need for this, providing you have looked after it well. Or use one of the general quick acting fertilizers like Growmore which can be applied at sowing time or even later.

Heavy manuring needs to be done about once in every four years and the best time to do it is just before you plant cabbages. This is why a rotation of crops is so important.

In addition, of course, some plants really do need special feeding and ' Harvest Gold ', which is the replacement for the old favourite ' Hoof and Horn ', is the ideal one for vegetables since it contains a high percentage of nitrogen. One feed is enough for the entire season since it is a slow release fertilizer. It should be applied in the Autumn before the season in which the crops are sown.

For tomatoes, there is a fast acting high potash liquid feed that contains seaweed extract with magnesium.

Dig in some manure about once every 4 years to help to ensure a good crop

GUIDE TO SOWING TIMES

VEGETABLE	MONTH	DEPTH
Artichoke, Jerusalem	February–March	4 inches
Bean, broad	November–April	3 inches
Bean, dwarf French	April–May	2 inches
Bean, runner	Mid-May–June	3 inches
Beetroot	Late-April–May	1½ inches
Brussels sprouts (late)	March–April	1 inch
Brussels sprouts (early)	September	1 inch
Cabbage (spring)	July–August	1 inch
Cabbage (summer)	April	1 inch
Cabbage (winter)	May	1 inch
Cabbage, red	September	1 inch
Carrot	March–July	½ inch
Cauliflower (early)	September	1 inch
Cauliflower (late)	March	1 inch
Cucumber, ridge	May–June	1½ inches
Leek	March	½ inch
Lettuce	March–July	Just cover
Marrow	Mid-May–June	1 inch
Onion	March	1 inch
Parsnip	March	½ inch
Peas	February–April	2 inches
Potatoes (early)	March–April	4 inches
Potatoes (main)	April–early May	4 inches
Radish	March–July	½ inch
Shallot	February	Tips showing
Spinach, beet	March–May	1½ inches
Swede	May–July	¾ inch
Turnip	March–June	1 inch

GUIDE TO PLANTING OUT

(Only those plants which are normally transplanted are shown here.)

Vegetable	Month	Distance Apart in Rows	Between Rows
Brussels sprouts (late)	May–June	2 feet	2 feet
Brussels sprouts (early)	April	2 feet	2 feet
Cabbage (spring)	October	1½ feet	1½ feet
Cabbage (summer)	June	1½ feet	1½ feet
Cabbage (winter)	June–July	2 feet	2 feet
Cabbage, red	March	2 feet	2 feet
Cauliflower (early)	October	2 feet	2 feet
Cauliflower (late)	April–May	2 feet	2 feet
Celery	June	1 foot	1½ feet
Cucumber, ridge	June	3 feet	
Leek	May–July	6 inches	1½ feet
Lettuce	April–July	9 inches	1 foot
Marrows	June	5–6 feet	
Tomato	June	2 feet	2 feet

ARTICHOKE – JERUSALEM
(Tubers are the edible portion)

Plant the tubers in February or March. Leave in the ground and lift as required during the winter. You can leave them in for several years but you will find they grow bigger and better if they are planted in rich new soil each year.

BROAD BEANS

It is worth remembering that if a few pods of the broad bean are allowed to mature on the plant, and later when the pods are black, they are shelled, the beans that are obtained provide seed for the next year's plants. They should be spread out and allowed to dry naturally and stored in a cool, dry place for sowing the following year. The same can be done with all the members of the bean family. It is also worth trying the same with peas. With seeds constantly becoming more expensive it is a paying proposition to provide seeds in this way for the following season.

Well manure the trench in Autumn. It is one of the first crops to be sown and can be placed next to the path for easy access if the soil is sticky. Mark each end of the manured trench with a short stick. The seeds may be sown any time between November and April. February is a good month to do it assuming that the ground is soft enough. There are two main types of broad beans, Windsors and Longpods. Longpods are usually planted for early cropping. Place the garden line across the plot from marker to marker and arrange the seeds diagonally, 9 inches on either side of it.

Press the seeds down with your thumb to a depth of 3 inches and fill in the holes with earth.

Broad beans are very prone to attack by black fly. Towards the end of May it will be necessary to pinch out the growing point at the top of the plant, and treat with insecticide to counter this pest.

Pick regularly as soon as the pods fill out and while the seeds are still soft.

BEANS – DWARF FRENCH

Sow in April or May in the same way as Broad Beans.
Press the seeds 2 inches deep into the soil. They should not
need any support. Pick while the pods are young and
tender.

BEANS – RUNNER

Sow as for Broad Beans but leave more room between
them and the adjoining crop because of the height to which
they grow. Seed may be sown any time between mid-May
and early July for succession. They can be supported by
sticks, canes or on netting to a height of over 6 ft.

Look out for black fly and spray if neccessary.

Runner beans need a great deal of water and this should
be supplied from the time the flowers begin to appear. Pick
and use while the pods are young and tender.

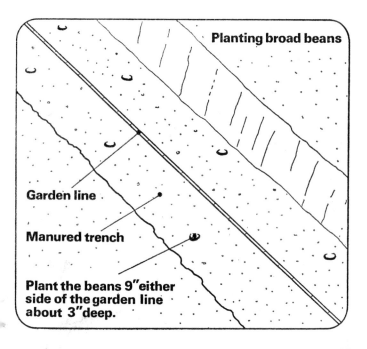

Planting broad beans

Garden line

Manured trench

Plant the beans 9"either
side of the garden line
about 3"deep.

BEETROOT

The crimson globe varieties of beetroot are the ones usually grown. They provide roots of a reasonable size, their only drawback being that occasionally they tend to run to seed. This will happen more frequently when sown too early. A beetroot that goes to seed can, however, still be used, so long as it is taken as soon as the tendency to bolt is noticed. On gathering beet it is advisable to screw off the top an inch or so from the crown to prevent bleeding. The tops should never be cut off.

Sow in drills 1½–2ins. deep in late April and in May.

They need soil that has been manured for the previous year's crop. New manure will cause the roots to fork.

Since this crop originates from a sea-shore plant it benefits from a dressing of salt. Agricultural salt or common salt may be used allowing ½ ounce to the square yard.

BRUSSELS SPROUTS

Sow in March or April to produce a crop the following February, and in September to pick the following October. Plant in rich firm ground about 30 inches apart when seedlings are eight weeks old. Mulch in late summer and start to pick the sprouts from early autumn onwards. Pick from the bottom of the plant as the sprouts mature.

CABBAGE

Good cabbage will only grow on rich, well-manured ground.

By planting a number of different varieties you can be sure of having cabbage all the year round. Start them off in seed beds and transplant when large enough, into rows 2 feet apart and with 18 inches between each plant.

Sow in April and they will be ready for use in summer; sow in May and you can cut them in autumn and winter; sow in July or August and they will be ready the following spring. There are some very quick maturing varieties such as Greyhound and Velocity that are most suitable for early use. The latter, in a good season, without being transplanted, will be ready for use twelve weeks after sowing the seed.

You don't have to grow them from seed, of course. You can buy young plants at the appropriate time.

Red Cabbage is also worth planting, both to use as a fresh vegetable and for pickling. Keep covered by nets if you are troubled by pigeons.

CARROTS

Sow thinly ½ inch deep in rows 1 foot apart from March to July. This will provide a continuous supply from May to October. Fresh manure promotes forked roots so the ground should have been manured for a crop during the previous season. Stump-rooted varieties are the best to start growing.

When the plants are 2–3 inches tall thin them out to 3 inches apart. At this stage the crop is liable to be attacked by the carrot fly, which lays its eggs on the young root. The grubs that hatch out feed from the root and kill the plant. To prevent this, dust along the row with calomel dust, especially after thinning out.

CAULIFLOWER

Sow seed for early summer varieties in March or April and for autumn varieties in late April or early May. Transplant the seedlings when they are about 8 weeks old, spacing them 2 feet apart.

Cauliflowers are hungry plants. They need very rich, well-manured soil and plenty of water.

CELERY

This is not an easy crop to grow. It is most important to transplant the seedlings at exactly the right time and for this reason it is easier to buy young plants than it is to raise from seed. You should also be sure to select the self-blanching variety which will not require trenching.

CUCUMBER

Frame cucumbers will produce a very good crop but they do require a lot of attention. Ridge cucumbers, however, need only the minimum of looking after. Sow the seeds in groups of three, between May and June, leaving spaces of 3 feet between each group. Remove the two weakest seedlings from each group. Keep well watered and mulch well.

LEEKS

Sow seed very thinly and only $\frac{1}{2}$ inch deep in March on well-manured ground. Thin out in late June or early July to 6 inches apart. The thinnings should be planted out in holes 6 inches deep and 18 inches between rows. Earth up the stems as they grow so that you get a longer length

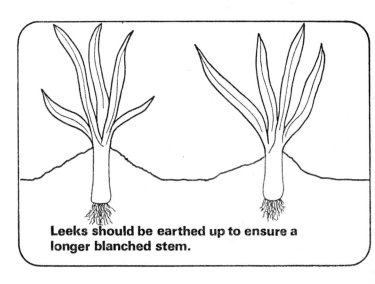

Leeks should be earthed up to ensure a longer blanched stem.

of blanched stem. This crop should be left in the ground when winter comes and the roots lifted as required.

LETTUCE

Lettuce likes a rich soil with plenty of moisture. Start sowing seed in March and repeat every two weeks right through until July so that you are able to use them from June to October. When sowing, the seed should be only just covered with soil. Lettuce can be set out between rows of dwarf beans or peas, or inter-cropped with the late maturing cabbages or cauliflower. The Cos lettuce grows taller than the Cabbage variety and the modern type is self-blanching.

MARROW

Plant 1 or 2 seeds to a pot in April and transplant at the end of May. The marrow bed should be prepared by digging out a pit 1 to $1\frac{1}{2}$ feet deep and, say, 3 feet square. This should accommodate 8 or 9 plants eventually. The pit is then filled with manure to within 6 inches of the top and trampled down. Cover the manure with fine soil in such a way that the whole bed is slightly hollowed. This makes watering easier throughout the growing period.

Protect the seeds with a cloche for the first few days. Keep well watered and well manured.

Alternatively, start seeds off in a small well-manured bed which has been specially prepared for growing marrows. Sow from the middle to the end of May. Pinch out leader shoots when the plant is about 17 inches long and so encourage the growth of side shoots. Pick the marrows when they are about 8 inches long, otherwise new ones will not form.

MUSTARD AND CRESS

Sow every 2–3 weeks in small beds of finely sifted soil.

If you wish to cut and serve them together then sow the Cress seeds 4 days earlier than the mustard. During the colder months, mustard and cress grows quite well in small boxes kept under glass.

ONIONS

Can be raised from seed sown in the autumn or spring or from sets sown in the spring. The plot should be prepared in the autumn and it is advisable to give deep trenching to provide thorough drainage and to enrich the soil. When the seedlings are large enough to handle they should be thinned out to 6 inches apart and given liquid manure once a fortnight. The thinnings which are removed can be used as spring onions for salads. All feeding or watering should be stopped by August to allow the bulbs to finish ripening. For use in the kitchen, the small to medium sized onions are more suitable. To this end it is as well to be careful not to over-feed. It is also worth noting that the very large onion, in general, does not keep as well, or as long, as the smaller ones. The tops should be bent over to prevent seeding once maturity has been reached. Lift towards the end of September and dry them off in a cool airy place before storing.

PARSNIP

This is a seed which germinates very slowly and it is important that a fresh supply is purchased each year. Seeds should be sown in March in ground which was manured for a previous crop. Thin out, leaving plants 9–12 inches apart. Feed with liquid manure during the growing season.

Parsnips improve in the frost so they can be left in the ground through the winter and taken up more or less as required.

PEAS

Peas are listed in catalogues as early, maincrop or late. The early varieties are quickest to come to maturity. The late ones take longer from sowing to gathering. Peas also vary considerably in the height to which they grow. Since the taller ones need more in the way of support they are perhaps a little more trouble to cultivate; the popular varieties are those which grow from $1\frac{1}{2}$ to 2 feet in height.

Peas should be sown over a well-manured trench in the same way as Broad Beans. Place the garden line across the plot where the peas are to be planted. Arrange the seeds along the line in sets of 5 as on a domino. Press each down with the thumb to a depth of 2 inches and then fill in the holes.

Protect with short sticks carrying black cotton about 3 inches from the ground. If you do this immediately after sowing it will provide protection from the birds throughout the early growing period when they are particularly vulnerable.

To make sure that you have sweet tender peas from the end of May until early autumn plant early, mid-season and late varieties. First sowing should be made between January and March. Keep the soil moist and as soon as the plants begin to develop surround them with netting supported by canes or with stakes. Pick when the pods are well filled and firm.

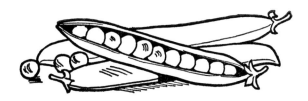

POTATOES

Potatoes are classed as Early, Second Early and Maincrop. The essential differences are in the time taken to come to eating readiness from the day of planting. Early potatoes are the quickest and in a good season are ready for trying about 13 weeks from the time of planting. Maincrop potatoes, however, need a much longer period for growth and will not be ready for digging up and storing until they have been in the ground at least 17 weeks.

Another choice that has to be made is whether to grow white varieties or potatoes with pink eyes or red skins. The latter are very popular and their flavour preferred by many people. White varieties, like Arran Pilot and Majestic, do, however, produce a much better crop and are less likely to attack from pests such as wireworm and leather-jackets which can leave the crop riddled with holes.

For the best results let the tubers start to sprout before you plant them but leave only 2 shoots about 1 inch long on each plant. The remainder should be rubbed off. Have rows running from north to south so that both sides of each row receives the same amount of sunlight. Planting can begin towards the end of March, 4 inches deep and 12 inches apart in manured trenches placed 2½ feet from each other. As foliage appears, earth up about 3 inches and a further 3 inches about 1 month later.

Start using early varieties from June and maincrop in August. Any still in the ground in October should be lifted and stored.

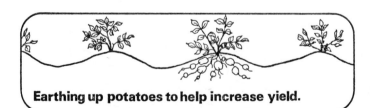

Earthing up potatoes to help increase yield.

RADISH

Sow from March–July either very thinly about $\frac{1}{2}$ inch deep or in drills 6 inches apart. Keep the soil moist and occasionally use a liquid manure. Radishes are ready to eat within a month of sowing and they are, in fact, the easiest crop of all to grow.

SHALLOT

The most successful method of planting shallots is to make holes with the trowel, line the holes with a little silver sand, and set the bulbs so that just the tip shows. Feed with liquid manure. Planting can start in February and they are ready to use when the leaves turn yellow and wither.

SPINACH BEET

This is a very easy crop to grow. Sow $1\frac{1}{2}$ inches deep. One sowing will provide for a long period but pick before it runs to seed.

SWEDE

Sow in May $\frac{3}{4}$ inch deep and thin out to 6 inches apart as soon as the seedlings are large enough to handle. Keep well watered to prevent stringiness. Use when the size of a tennis ball. The purple top varieties are best.

TOMATO

This can be grown out of doors in the South and West but not as a rule in the North or Midlands.

Choose a sunny spot, preferably against a south or west facing wall or fence. Plants should be 18 inches apart and they need to be kept well watered and mulched. Tie the plants to stout stakes. When four trusses of fruit have set, pinch out the main growing point. Pick the fruit as it ripens, starting from the bottom of the plant and working upwards. Any fruit not ripened by September should be picked and ripened off in a sunny window.

TURNIP

Sow in early April 1 inch deep and thin out plants to 6 inches apart. The soil should be well limed and the young plants kept well watered so that they grow quickly. Use when they are the size of a golf ball or just a little larger. You can sow a winter variety in early July and these can be left in the ground and used as required.

Month by Month in the Garden

JANUARY

Usually the weather is too cold to do very much outdoor work. If you can do any digging, however, just turn the ground over and leave the soil in clods to be broken down by the frost. If the ground it too hard for digging then just spread manure over the top and leave it there.

Spend any other leisure time planning out in detail what you are going to grow and just where you are going to plant everything. Keep in mind the importance of crop rotation. Finally, order your seed potatoes, vegetable seeds and fertilizers. When your seed potatoes arrive, sort them into shallow trays with the crown or rose end upwards and keep them in a cool dry place with plenty of light. Make sure they will come to no harm from frost. If necessary cover them over in severe weather, but do not leave them like this very long since it will tend to produce long, white, weak shoots. If the severe weather continues, move the trays to a cool place into which the frost cannot penetrate.

You may be wondering just how much seed of each type you should order. Seed packets rarely shows the weight of the seed enclosed but the following table may guide you since you can always weigh the contents of the packet yourself. In the case of potatoes, the ideal potato set weighs 2 ounces so you will get 6 or 7 sets to the pound. Early varieties should be planted about 12 inches apart, others 15 inches apart, so from this you should be able to work out how many to order.

QUANTITY GUIDE FOR SEEDS

Broad Beans: 1 pt. will sow 100 ft.
Beans *French*: ½ pt. sows 150 ft.
Beans *Runner*: ½ pt. sows 50 ft.
Beetroot: 1 oz. will sow 90 ft.
Carrot: ½ oz. will sow 100 ft.
Leek: ¼ oz. will sow 180 feet.
Lettuce: ¼ oz. each variety enough for successive sowing for summer and winter supplies.

Onion: 1 oz. will sow 150 ft.
Parsnip: ½ oz. will sow 100 ft.
Peas: 1 pt. will sow 90 ft.
Radish: 1 oz. will sow a full season's supply.
Shallot: 25 bulbs will give a row 15 ft. long.
Swede: ½ oz. will sow 100 ft.
Turnip: ½ oz. will sow 100 ft.

FEBRUARY

If you didn't manage to dig over your vegetable plot in the autumn or during January then try and get it done as soon as possible now. There are often quite severe frosts during February and these are wonderful for breaking up the newly-turned soil.

Don't try working the soil when it is very wet and sticky and certainly don't try putting in seeds or plants when the ground is wet or heavy since they will rot instead of germinating and even those that do survive will be only poor quality.

Towards the end of the month, onion sets and shallots can be planted. The seed potatoes for early varieties should now have shoots an inch or so long on them but it is advisable to leave planting them until mid-March. Broad beans and the early varieties of peas can go in now and it is the right time to divide up rhubarb roots and re-plant.

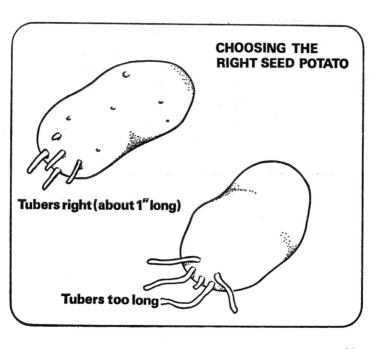

CHOOSING THE
RIGHT SEED POTATO

Tubers right (about 1" long)

Tubers too long

MARCH

This should be a very busy month in the garden. Seeds of most vegetables which mature above ground such as greens of all kinds, should be sown towards the end of the month given favourable weather conditions. If you can arrange to sow your seeds just prior to a shower then this is first class. Rain is far better for them than watering. If, however, the ground is very dry then it should be well watered using the fine rose on the watering can an hour or so before sowing.

If you haven't already done so make sure you sow parsnips, peas, summer lettuce, radishes, parsley, onions and potatoes all before the end of the month. Lettuce and radish should be sown again in a few weeks' time to make sure you have a continuous crop.

As soon as seedlings appear above ground and are large enough to handle, thin them out leaving the strongest ones to grow to maturity. If you don't thin out properly then all the plants will be stunted and useless.

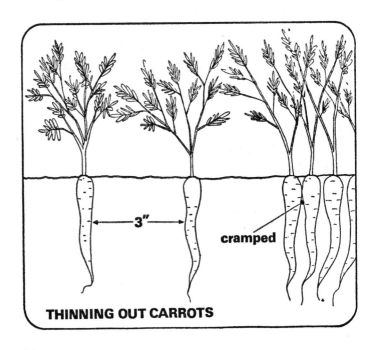

3"

cramped

THINNING OUT CARROTS

APRIL

Finish sowing seeds you may have forgotten or not been able to sow during March.

Everything starts to grow in April, the weeds in particular, and unless you use your Dutch hoe regularly and often the weeds will overtake the plants. Remember you only need to hoe the surface between growing crops; don't hoe deeply and take care not to damage the young growing plants. Towards the end of the month make second or even third sowings of such things as radish, carrot and lettuce to make sure you have a supply right through the summer months ahead. French beans can also be sown, provided the weather is reasonably mild.

MAY

This is another very busy month. Seedlings must be thinned out, potatoes earthed up and peas and beans will benefit from mulching. Pinch out the topmost bud from your broad beans and this will help in controlling the black fly which so often infests this plant.

A late frost in May can do a great deal of harm to your potatoes so if there is any signs of frost cover the young plants over lightly with soil if they are small enough for this to be effective. Otherwise have a very large sheet of polythene handy for covering the whole potato plot at night remember this *must* be removed early the next morning.

Runner beans should now be planted but make sure the soil is not too wet for them and decide whether you are going to grow them in rows or in a circle round a central stake as described on p. 18.

Don't forget to sow some marrow seeds, put in celery plants and right at the end of the month put in tomato plants.

Don't forget to keep your compost heap going. Weeds, lawn mowings and any other available waste should be collected and the heap built up and allowed to rot down.

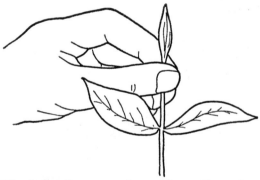

Pinch out the young broad bean tips when the plants are about 3ft high.

JUNE

Potatoes will now need a second earthing up. If you haven't planted any greens for winter picking now is the time to put in plants of Brussels sprouts, savoys and any other varieties you like.

Main crop carrots, swedes and turnips can all be sown towards the end of the month.

Beet, carrots, parsnips, lettuce and spinach will all need to be thinned out and those that were thinned out in May should be given a feed of liquid fertilizer.

Keep an eye on your tomato plants and pinch out the side shoots, keep them well watered and feed them occasionally with liquid fertilizer. When watering remember you should allow about ½ gallon to each plant. If you have rain water available so much the better.

Don't let up on the hoeing during June, the weeds are still growing fast. Make sure you are picking peas and beans as soon as they reach perfection and don't leave lettuce to run to seed. It is best to do your picking first thing in the morning or in the late evening. If you gather them during the heat of the day they will appear limp.

Pinch out the side shoots.

JULY

Leeks, Onions and Green Crops for next winter should all receive special attention this month. Plant out winter cabbage and if the ground is very dry water in each hole before you put the young plants in. Make sure they are planted very firmly. If you are putting in Brussels sprouts, remember they like very firm ground and it's a good idea to earth up around the stems about a week after planting.

This is your last chance to sow French beans and peas in order to pick a late crop but it is well worth doing so. Keep them well watered.

Check over your root crops such as carrots and turnips to make sure they are not overcrowding each other. Thin out if necessary otherwise you will not get any roots of worthwhile size.

Don't forget to keep your compost heap going with all the waste vegetable growth, grass cuttings and so on, since this will produce valuable humus for digging into your soil in the autumn.

This is the best time for planting out leeks. Using a dibber, make a hole at least six inches deep and drop the plant in, put some water into the hole first and then enough soil to keep the plant firm.

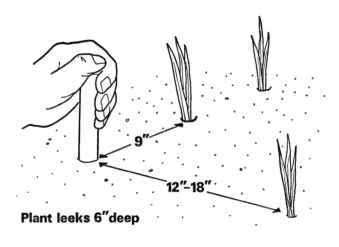

Plant leeks 6″ deep

AUGUST

Frequent picking of runner beans will encourage the plants to go on producing right up until the first frost. If you have an abundant crop remember they are worth freezing for winter use, or you can pickle some in salt if you haven't room for them in your deep freeze cabinet.

Feed your cauliflower with liquid manure once or twice a week and cut them when the heads are really firm and white. Once they start to turn yellow they lose both their flavour and eye-appeal.

It's important to keep hoeing between growing plants to keep the weeds under control and as ground becomes vacant it's a good idea to dig it over and manure it in preparation for next season, or to plant greens for winter and early spring use.

Early beet should be ready for pulling, if you leave it in the ground too long it will become woody and stringy, remember.

Summer turnips should be ready to use and any early-sown carrots should be pulled and used. Marrows and tomatoes should be picked as they ripen. If you haven't already pinched out the main growing shoots of these plants then do so now, otherwise the fruit already formed will not have a chance to mature before the frost arrives.

Pinch out the main growing shoots.

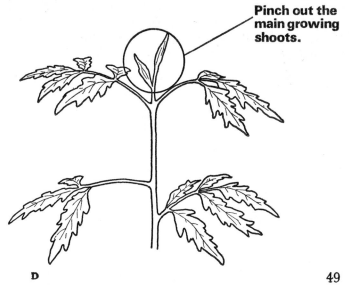

SEPTEMBER

Your onions should be ready for picking. After you have dug them up lay them out on wire netting so that they can dry off thoroughly.

Keep a close watch on your tomato plants, unless you pinch out any shoots or late forming fruit, the existing fruit will not ripen quickly enough. Remove seed pods from dwarf and runner beans and this will encourage these plants to go on producing right up until the first frost.

If the weather is dry, vegetable marrows, tomatoes and cucumbers will need watering daily and occasionally they should be given liquid manure. Choose a dry spell to lift potatoes, and leave them spread out in the open air to dry before storing them in sacks or barrels.

Don't put the potato haulms (tops) onto your compost heap if they show any signs of disease or blight. Instead burn them.

Fully developed marrows can be gathered and stored for winter use providing you handle them with extreme care so as not to damage or bruise them in any way. The best way to store them is to hang them from the ceiling in nets.

Any tomatoes which have not yet ripened should be picked, stored on trays with strips of newspaper between them so that they do not touch, and then stored somewhere warm yet dark. Examine them from time to time and remove any which may have split or show signs of decay, otherwise bring them out a few at a time for ripening off as required.

OCTOBER

If you haven't completed the lifting of potatoes then this should be attended to as soon as possible since once the frost has got at them they will not be suitable for eating. Any carrots or beets still in the ground should also be lifted.

October is the month for giving your vegetable garden a good clean up. Keep the hoe going between any plants still in the ground.

The compost heap that you have been building all year should now prove invaluable since everything should have rotted down and be ready for spreading over your garden to ensure the ground is rich for planting in next spring. Before you do this, however, clear the ground thoroughly of all weeds and dead foliage. Start a new compost heap with this. Don't put any diseased, or pest infected waste onto the compost heap but burn it instead.

Early planted Brussels sprouts should now be ready for picking; start at the bottom and clear the stems of sprouts as they become large enough. If you have a very large crop of potatoes you may wish to consider storing some of them in clamps, that is in a deep trench in the ground that is lined with straw to protect the potatoes from frost and damp.

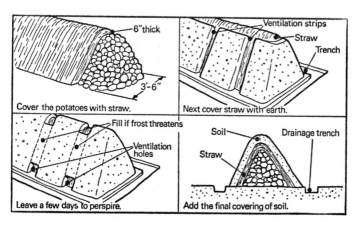

DIAGRAM OF A CLAMP

NOVEMBER

Before the really bad weather sets in, dig over your vegetable garden and leave it to lie rough through the next month or so. The frosts and snow and winter weather generally will break up the heavy clods, disperse the nutrition from the manure or compost you have spread over it and do all the hard work of preparing the soil for next year's crops. If you have very heavy ground, dig in some sand to help lighten it. Apart from this and general tidying up, there is not a great deal you can do in the garden during November.

Sweep up any dead leaves and store them in a compost heap, covering them with loam from time to time to help them decay more quickly, and to prevent them from being blown about.

From time to time check over your stores of root vegetables and remove any that show the slightest signs of decay before they can affect any others.

If you have a heavy soil dig in some sand.

DECEMBER

Not very much to be done out of doors this month, in fact many gardeners make a point of thoroughly cleaning and greasing their tools and hanging them up for a few weeks. While doing this, check to see if there are any replacements needed or any new tools you feel you particularly need. Christmas is only just around the corner so it may not be too late to drop some hints. Be specific about the type you want, though, as it is a false economy to have inferior quality tools or ones which are not suitable for the job you need them to do. If you would prefer to choose your own tools, and try them out in the shop to get the ' feel ' of them before buying, then it may be better to drop hints concerning other things for your garden, such as books on specialized cultivation, or seeds of new varieties of vegetables you would like to try.

ARTICHOKE (JERUSALEM)

Allow 6–8 ounces per portion.
Scrub, peel quickly, plunge into cold water, add a few drops of lemon juice or vinegar to prevent discolouration.

Cook in boiling water for 30 minutes until soft. Drain, garnish with chopped parsley. Serve with melted butter or white sauce.

BROAD BEANS

4–8 ounces per serving.
Shell beans and cook in boiling salted water 20-30 minutes until soft. Serve on own or with parsley sauce.

BEANS – FRENCH

4–8 ounces per serving.
Top, tail and string the beans then leave whole or slice. Cook in boiling salted water 15-20 minutes. Remove any scum that rises to the surface during cooking. Drain and toss with salt and pepper and knob of butter.

BEANS – RUNNER

4–8 ounces per serving.
Top, tail and string the beans. Slice thinly. Cook in boiling salted water 15-20 minutes until soft. Remove any scum that rises during cooking. Drain and toss with salt, pepper and a knob of butter. For a pleasant change, try boiling an onion about the size of a golf ball in with beans when cooking them.

BEETROOT

Allow 4–6 ounces when served as a vegetable.
Screw off the tops $1\frac{1}{2}$ inches from the crown. Wash thoroughly taking care not to break the skin or they will 'bleed' when boiled. Boil in salted water until they are tender—about 2 hours. Peel off skin, slice or cube. Serve hot with white sauce or cold, slice with a little vinegar.

BRUSSELS SPROUTS

4–6 ounces per serving.
Wash, remove discoloured leaves and cut a cross in the stalks. Cook in boiling salted water 10-20 minutes until soft. Drain. Add salt and pepper and a knob of butter and re-heat for a few seconds.

CABBAGE

4 ounces per serving.
Remove coarse outer leaves. Cut in half and remove hard centre stalk. Wash thoroughly, shred finely, cook rapidly in 1 inch boiling water 15-20 minutes. Drain well, toss in knob of butter, pepper and salt.

CARROTS

4–6 ounces per serving.
Trim off leaves, scrape lightly with a sharp knife. Small new carrots can be cooked whole. Simmer in salted water for 15-20 minutes. Serve tossed with a little butter, pepper and chopped parsley. They will also combine with parsnip, swede, turnip as a boiled vegetable. They are ideal in stews, casseroles, etc.

CAULIFLOWER

Allow a medium size cauliflower for four servings.
Remove coarse outer leaves. Cut a cross in the base of the stem. Wash well and cook stem side down in fast-boiling salted water for 20-30 minutes. Drain well and serve coated with white sauce or cheese sauce. Or, divide into florets and cook in fast-boiling salted water for 15 minutes. Serve tossed with butter and a sprinkling of pepper.

CELERY

2–3 sticks per serving.

Wash, scrub and cut into even lengths. Cook in boiling salted water 30–50 minutes or until tender. Drain well, serve with white parsley sauce or cheese sauce. Coarse sticks can be chopped and added to stews and soups.

LEEKS

1–3 leeks per serving.

Remove coarse outer leaves, cut off roots and tops. Wash, splitting them down the centre to within 1 inch of base to ensure all grit is removed. If necessary, cut them right through. Shred, then cook in boiling water 20-30 minutes. Drain thoroughly. Serve coated with white sauce or cheese sauce. Shredded leeks can also be fried or added to a stew.

LETTUCE

This is usually served as a salad but the thinnings can be cooked in the same way as cabbage. When cooked they are similar in taste and appearance to spinach and can be served with a white sauce.

MARROW

6 ounces per serving.
Peel, remove seeds and cut flesh in even-sized pieces. Cook in boiling salted water for about 20 minutes. Drain well. Serve with a white sauce or a cheese sauce. Can also be roasted in the dripping round the meat or stuffed and baked.

ONIONS

4–6 ounces per serving.
Skin and trim. Cut up if desired. Cook in boiling salted water 30-45 minutes. Drain and use as required.
Onions may also be fried, braised, stuffed or baked, or used in stews and casseroles.

PARSNIPS

6–8 ounces per serving.
Wash, peel quarter and remove the hard centre core. Cut in slices, strips or dice. Cook in boiling salted water 30-40 minutes. Drain and toss in butter, salt and pepper.
To roast : par boil for five minutes in salted water, drain and put in fat around the meat joint for 1 hour.

PEAS

2–3 ounces (after shelling) per serving.
Shell, wash, place in boiling salted water with 1 level teaspoon sugar and a sprig of mint. Cook 12–15 minutes. Drain, remove mint, toss with a knob of butter.

POTATOES

6–8 ounces per portion.
Peel thinly. New potatoes can be scraped. Cook in boiling salted water 15-30 minutes. Drain. Serve whole or mashed with butter.
They can also be baked, roasted, fried or sautéd.

SWEDES

4–6 ounces per serving.
Peel thickly, cut up, cook in boiling salted water 30–60 minutes. Serve mashed with butter and seasoning.
They can also be used in stews or boiled in combination with carrots, parsnips or turnips.

TURNIPS

4–6 ounces per serving.
If young leave whole, older ones should be sliced or diced. Peel, cook in boiling salted water 20-30 minutes. Serve tossed in butter or top of the milk or with a white sauce.

Sowing and Harvesting - SPRING & SUMMER

Legend: Sowing (S), Harvesting (H), Planting (P), S/H = sowing and harvesting in same month

VARIETY	MAR	APR	MAY	JUNE	JULY	AUG	SEPT
ARTICHOKE (Jerusalem)	S						H
BROAD BEANS	S	S			H	H	
BEANS (Dwarf french)		S	S	H	H	H	H
BEANS (Runner)			S	S	H	H	H
BEETROOT		S	S	S	H	H	H
BRUSSELS SPROUT		S	S				H
CABBAGE	S	S	S	H	S/H	S/H	H
CARROT	S	S/H	S/H	S/H	S/H	H	H
CAULIFLOWER	S	S	S	S	H	H	H
CELERY			S	S			H
CUCUMBER				S	S/H	H	H
LEEKS	S	S					
LETTUCE	S	S	S/H	S/H	S/H	S/H	H
MARROW			S	S	H	H	H
MUSTARD & CRESS	S	S/H	S/H	S/H	S/H	S/H	S/H
ONIONS	S	S				H	H
PARSNIP	S						
PEAS	S	S	S	S/H	S/H	H	H
POTATOES	S	S	S		H	H	H
RADISH	S	S/H	S/H	S/H	S/H	S/H	S/H
SHALLOT	S	S			H	H	H
SPINACH BEET	S	S	S/H	S/H	S/H	H	H
SWEDE				S	S	S	
TOMATO				P	H	H	H
TURNIP	S	S	S/H	S/H	S/H	H	H

Sowing and Harvesting - AUTUMN & WINTER

VARIETY	SEPT	OCT	NOV	DEC	JAN	FEB
ARTICHOKE (Jerusalem)	harvesting	harvesting	harvesting	harvesting	harvesting	
BROAD BEANS		sowing	sowing			
BEANS (Dwarf french)	harvesting	harvesting				
BEANS (Runner)	harvesting	harvesting				
BEETROOT	harvesting	harvesting				
BRUSSELS SPROUT	sowing/harvesting	harvesting	harvesting	harvesting	harvesting	harvesting
CABBAGE	harvesting	harvesting				
CARROT	harvesting	harvesting				
CAULIFLOWER	harvesting	harvesting	harvesting			
CELERY	harvesting	harvesting	harvesting			
CUCUMBER						
LEEKS		harvesting	harvesting	harvesting	harvesting	harvesting
LETTUCE	harvesting	harvesting				
MARROW	harvesting	harvesting				
MUSTARD & CRESS	sowing/harvesting	sowing/harvesting	harvesting			
ONIONS	harvesting	harvesting				
PARSNIP			harvesting	harvesting	harvesting	harvesting
PEAS	harvesting	harvesting				
POTATOES	harvesting	harvesting				
RADISH	sowing/harvesting	harvesting				
SHALLOT	harvesting					
SPINACH BEET	harvesting	harvesting				
SWEDE		harvesting	harvesting	harvesting		
TOMATO						
TURNIP	harvesting	harvesting				

HARVESTING

SOWING

PLANNING THE PLOT

VARIETY	JAN	FEB	MAR	APR	MAY	JUN	JULY	AUG	SEPT	OCT	NOV	DEC	JAN	FEB	A 10ft row	Distance between rows	Final spacing in row
ARTICHOKE (Jerusalem)		O	O						H	H	H	H	H		12 lbs	2½ ft	15 ins
BROAD BEANS		O	O	O			H	H		O	O				5 lbs	double rows 3ft apart	9 ins
BEANS (Dwarf french)				O	O	H	H	H	H	H					4-5 lbs	1-2ft	1ft
BEANS (Runner)					O	O	H	H	H	H					40 lbs	double rows 5ft apart	1ft
BEETROOT				O	O	O	O/H	H	H	H					9 lbs	15 ins	9 ins
BRUSSELS SPROUT	H	H	O/H	O					O/H	H	H	H	H	H	5 lbs	2½-3ft	30 ins
CABBAGE			O	O	O	H	O/H	O/H	H	H					6-7 heads	2ft	18 ins
CARROT			O	O/H	O/H	O/H	O/H	H	H	H					5-6 lbs	1ft	3 ins
CAULIFLOWER			O	O	O	O	H	H	H	H	H				5 heads	2ft	2ft
CELERY				O	O				H	H	H				10-12 lbs	9 ins	9 ins
CUCUMBER					O	O/H	H	H							3 Plants	3ft	3ft
LEEKS		O	O						H	H	H	H	H	H	7-8 lbs	18 ins	6 ins
LETTUCE			O	O	O/H	O/H	O/H	O/H	H	H					10-12 heads	9-12ins	9-12ins
MARROW					O	O	H	H	H	H					10-20 lbs	4-5ft	2ft
MUSTARD & CRESS			O	O/H	O/H	O/H	O/H	O/H	O/H	O/H	H				See instructions on seed packet		
ONIONS			O	O				H	H	H					8 lbs	1ft	6 ins
PARSNIP			O							H	H	H	H	H	7½ lbs	12-15 ins	9-12 ins
PEAS			O	O	O	O/H	O/H	H	H	H					5 lbs	8 ins	2-3 ins
POTATOES			O	O	O		H	H	H	H					15 lbs	2½ ft	12 ins
RADISH			O	O/H	O/H	O/H	O/H	O/H	O/H	H					3 lbs	6 ins	2 ins
SHALLOT		O	O	O			H	H	H						25 lbs	1ft	6 ins
SPINACH BEET			O	O	O/H	O/H	O/H	H	H	H					8-10 Plants	1ft	6-8 ins
SWEDE					O	O	O		H	H	H				8 lbs	15-18 ins	6 ins
TOMATO	O	O			P	H	H	H							25 lbs	3ft	15 ins
TURNIP			O	O	O/H	O/H	O/H	H	H	H					8 lbs	15 ins	6 ins

H HARVESTING

O SOWING

P PLANTING